Scenes and Wonders

Christian drama with a sense of humour

Paul Powell

National Society/Church House Publishing

National Society/Church House Publishing
Church House,
Great Smith Street,
London SW1P 3NZ

ISBN 0 7151 4843 5

First published in 1994 by The National Society and Church House
Publishing

Performing Rights

Photocopying

Text design and typesetting by The National Society
Cover design by Rhino Design
Printed in Scotland by Indeprint Print Production Services

Contents

The author and publishers would like to thank the following people for their help in road-testing many of the sketches in this collection:

Roger Bird and Southborough Methodist Church Sunday School, Tunbridge Wells

Clive Bond and St Michael's Acting Group, Towcester

Brendan Harnett and various classes from Bishop Douglass School, East Finchley

Maggie Scholes and Holy Trinity Junior Church, Peterborough

Indulgent Bit by the Author

These sketches are written for teenagers and students, but they should appeal to just about everybody. They can be used in school assemblies, church services, or for street evangelism. Each piece sets out to communicate Christian faith and Christian living in a humorous and vibrant manner. The various combinations of cast sizes, running times, and settings mean there should be something for everyone.

This collection comes as a response to the chasm between the humour we so often present in the Church and that we enjoy on television and radio. Having experience in both media, as a writer for *Spitting Image* and *Week Ending*, my aim is to produce drama with a Christian perspective that is as enjoyable as mainstream entertainment. The timeless message of the Gospel is expressed in a manner relevant for today's pop culture, using familiar situations, characters, and language. The audience is encouraged to identify with the scenes, and to respond to them.

To that end, the material is designed to provoke and to challenge. Often a piece will establish a debate without resolving it. There are two reasons for this. Firstly, the tensions and complexities of life simply cannot be adequately sorted out in a five-minute piece of drama. Secondly, each sketch is intended as a springboard for discussion. I want to open minds – allow people to reach their own decisions – rather than impose my own views.

It is my firm belief that humour is a gift from God that makes us question our behaviour and that of others. It strips away artifice, hypocrisy, and absurdity, revealing essential truths and values. The sketches may veer towards farce, but their intention is always to provoke and to inform. And, most importantly, to give glory to God.

I would like to express my gratitude to my editor for her invaluable help, the various groups who road-tested material, my long-suffering flat mates, and the Reverend Paul Williams for theological advice and bacon sandwiches.

This book is dedicated to my family.

Paul Powell
June 1994

The Light in the Darkness

This sketch is based on John 1.5 – a fascinating verse crammed full of meaning. Here we see the human condition – blind, self-satisfied, and ignorant. Ultimately self-destructive. The light which is offered represents truth, knowledge, and freedom – the salvation of Christ. Sadly, the clarity and brilliance of the Gospel are too frequently rejected.

NB The blindfolds should look dark, but be made of material light enough for the actors to see through – thus avoiding genuine accidents.

Cast   Stephen
Alison
Mark
Dawn
Extras

Props   Torch
Blindfolds

In semi-darkness, a group of people wearing blindfolds are stumbling around. They trip, bump, lose things, and knock things over. It's truly anarchic. Stephen enters without a blindfold carrying a torch. While Stephen speaks, everyone continues to shuffle about. He walks amongst them, shining the light around.

Stephen   Look, everyone – our problems are over!

Alison   Who is it?

Stephen   It's me – Stephen. I can see!

Mark   What are you talking about?

Dawn   You can see?! What's that mean?

Stephen   If you take off your blindfold, you'll find out.

Alison   Blindfold? What blindfold?

Mark   He's talking rubbish!

Dawn   We're perfectly alright – leave us alone.

Stephen   I've been given a light. I can find my way around. Everything's much clearer – and much, much easier.

Alison   Stephen – what are you talking about?

Mark   What on earth is a light?

Dawn	What good is a light?
Alison	Why should we need a light?
Stephen	Because it's much safer. Because it's much nicer. And because with a light everything makes a lot more sense.
Mark	You're mad, you are.
Dawn	You're round the twist!
Alison	Go and talk to the trees, Mr Loopy!
Stephen	But you need help. You'll get lost. You'll get hurt.
Mark	Rubbish! We're perfectly alright. We're happy and we're safe.
Dawn	So get lost.
Alison	And take your light with you!
Stephen	*(Sighs)* Alright. I did my best. Take care. *(He exits mournfully, passing through the audience.)*
Mark	Take care? Huh!
Dawn	Who did he think he was?
Alison	Talk about patronising!

One by one the people on-stage trip over or walk into walls. They fall to the ground in a terrible heap, moaning and groaning. The stage goes completely dark.

A Bag of Happiness

We live in a very consumerist society. Advertisers tell us we can achieve importance and self-satisfaction through the way we spend our money – that material goods equal happiness. This sketch attempts to put the record straight.

Cast   Shop Assistant (male or female)
Bob
Barbara

Props   Counter
Shopping list

The Shop Assistant is standing behind a counter as Bob and Barbara enter.

Bob and Barbara Good morning!

Assistant	Good morning! How can I help you?
Bob	This is Perrins Department Store?
Assistant	That's right, sir.
Barbara	The store that sells everything?
Assistant	That's right, madam . . . *(Spreading his arms widely)* . . . everything! From answerphones to xylophones – Perrins is the store for you!
Bob	Marvellous. In that case we'd like to buy some . . . let me see now . . . *(Unwraps shopping list from pocket and reads)* oh yes . . . happiness.
Assistant	I'm sorry?
Barbara	Some happiness. Not much – a small bag will do.
Assistant	You want a bag of happiness?!
Bob	That's right. Do you take Barclaycard?
Assistant	*(Looking professionally apologetic)* I'm afraid we don't sell happiness, sir.
Barbara	*(Disappointed)* Oh dear.
Bob	*(Looking upset, brow wrinkled)* That *is* a shame.

They look disconsolate for a moment or two, before looking at the list again.

Barbara   Can you order some?

Assistant   What? Happiness?!

Bob   Yes. Get some from the warehouse. Make Head Office buy a few crates.

Assistant   You don't understand. We don't stock happiness. You can't buy happiness.

Barbara   But this is Perrins! The store that sells . . .
(Spreading her arms widely)
. . . everything!

Assistant   Handkerchiefs – yes. Hairpins – yes. Hungarian hatstands – yes. But happiness – no.

Bob   Oh dear.

Barbara   That *is* a shame.

Bob and Barbara shrug their shoulders and look depressed, before looking at the list once again.

Bob   Do they have some in Marks & Spencer?

Assistant   No.

Barbara   What about John Menzies?

Assistant   No.

Bob   Sainsbury's?

Assistant   No! You can't buy happiness. It's impossible. Happiness is an abstract concept – it's intangible. It has no physical manifestation!

Barbara   Oh dear.

Bob   That *is* a shame.

Barbara shrugs her shoulders, and once again consults the list.

Barbara   In that case we'll have a box of . . .
(Reading)
. . . inner peace.

Assistant   *(Disbelieving)*
Inner Peace?!

Bob	Don't bother wrapping it – we'll have it now, please.
Barbara	Does it need batteries?
Assistant	I'm very sorry but you can't buy inner peace either.
Bob and Barbara	*(Looking quite annoyed)*
	Tsk! Tsk! Tsk!
Barbara	*(Consulting list)*
	How about freedom from guilt?
Assistant	No.
Bob	Forgiveness?
Assistant	*(Getting bored)*
	No.
Barbara	Love?
Assistant	*(Bored)*
	No.
Bob	Eternal life?
Assistant	*(Bored to tears)*
	No!
Barbara	Oh dear.
Bob	That *is* a shame.
Assistant	How about an answerphone? Or a xylophone?
Barbara	No thanks. The man on the radio specifically said happiness, inner peace, freedom from guilt . . .
Bob	Forgiveness, love, and eternal life.
Assistant	What man on the radio?
Barbara	The man on Sunday morning. He said all these things were freely available.
Bob	All you had to do is ask for them!
Assistant	This man – he wasn't a vicar, was he?
Barbara	*(Shrugging)*
	Well, we couldn't really tell. You can't see a dog-collar on the radio.
Assistant	Um. Was it the morning service you were listening to?

Bob   *(Scratching head and thinking deeply)*
                   Well – it was definitely in a church. There was an
                   organ and hymns and stuff . . .

Assistant   That explains it then. If you want happiness, inner
                   peace . . .

Barbara   Freedom from guilt, forgiveness . . .

Bob   Love, and eternal life . . .

Assistant   Then you'd best try the church up the road. I think
                   it's called *(insert name of host church)*.

Barbara   Oh right. Thank you.

Assistant   Talk to a fella called Jesus. He'll help you out.

Bob   Marvellous. Thanks very much.

Barbara   Very kind of you.

Assistant   Not at all. Glad to oblige.

Bob and Barbara start to walk off. Bob halts and turns to the assistant.

Bob   Actually – one more thing . . . ?

Assistant   Yes?

Bob   This church . . . do they do deliveries?

Partytime

This is a reworking of the Parable of the Great Banquet (Luke 14. 15-24) demonstrating how we allow earthly interests to keep us from heavenly ones. To that end I've tried to convey God's immeasurable generosity in a context that the audience will find relevant. As a consequence, that generosity has been somewhat simplified. Obviously Heaven is much, much more than a giant party – and eternal life is considerably more than a halted ageing process. But the message remains undiluted: our deepest commitment should be to God, and not to ourselves.

Cast   Professor
Kevin
Rachel
James
Sarah
Derek
Jean
Extras

Props   Broom
Glass
White coat
Glasses
Record bag
Hand-held video game

Kevin is sweeping the stage with a broom. The Professor enters excitedly, clutching a glass filled with coloured water. He is wearing a white coat, glasses, and sports a manic crop of hair.

Professor   Kevin! Kevin! I've done it! I've finally done it!

Kevin   What? You've sat through a whole episode of 'Neighbours'?

Professor   No – I've found the serum!
(Holds up glass)
The serum that halts the ageing process! Do you know what this means?

Kevin   Um . . .
(Scratching his head)
Horlicks going out of business?

Professor   No. People can live forever! They'll never grow old and they'll never die! We've beaten Death, Kevin. It's the greatest discovery of all mankind. We must celebrate at once!

Kevin   Oh. I'll put the kettle on, shall I?

Professor   No – I mean really celebrate. I want you to go out and invite all my friends to an enormous party. That way we can have a really good time, drink the serum, and then live forever!
(Spreads his arms in triumph)

Kevin   *(Rubbing his stomach)*
Will there be any cake, Professor?

Professor   Of course there will. It's going to be the greatest party ever.

Kevin   Better than Sally Sharp's fancy dress barbecue?

Professor   *(Nodding)*
Much better. Now don't hang about, Kevin – get out there and spread the good news!

Kevin   *(Reluctantly)*
Alright, alright. If I have to!

As the Professor exits stage-left, Rachel enters from stage-right clutching a record bag. Kevin waves to her.

Kevin   Hello, Rachel.

Rachel   Hello, Kevin. How are you?

Kevin   Very well thanks. Look – I've been sent by the Professor. There's a fantastic party happening and . . .
(Pointing)
. . . you're invited!

Rachel   What – now?

Kevin   Yes – now!

Rachel   Sorry, Kevin – I can't come. I'm far too busy.

Kevin   *(Amazed)*
What?

Rachel   *(Holds up record bag)*
I've just bought a Simply Red album and I'm off to listen to it.

13

Kevin   But this is far better than a Simply Red album!

Rachel   How do you know? You haven't heard it yet!

As Rachel exits stage-left, James enters from stage-right playing a hand-held video game.

Kevin   Hello, James.

James   *(Absorbed in his game)*
Hi, Kevin.

Kevin   Look – I've been sent by the Professor. There's a fantastic party happening and . . .
(Pointing)
. . . you're invited!

James   *(Still looking at his game)*
Sorry, Kev – I really can't spare the time.

Kevin   Why not?

James   Well, I've just reached level 242 on this video game.

Kevin   What?

James   I'm 2,000 points away from an extra life and I've found the hidden password to the Banquet Hall.

Kevin   But if you come with me, you can have an eternal life – and a real banquet!

James   Hmmm.
(Looking up at last)
Has it got a CD mega drive?

Kevin   *(Shaking head)*
Not as such.

James   Hidden passwords?

Kevin   *(Shaking head and looking apologetic)*
We hadn't planned any, no.

James   Humph! Sounds far too easy. I think I'll stay here.

As James walks off stage-left, still engrossed in his game, Sarah enters stage-right adjusting her hair and clothes.

Kevin   Hello, Sarah.

Sarah   Hello, Kevin. What's up?

Kevin	Look – I've been sent by the Professor. There's a fantastic party happening and . . . *(Pointing)* . . . you're invited!
Sarah	Sorry, Kevin – I can't make it right now. I'm too busy.
Kevin	What?
Sarah	I've just got myself a new boyfriend and we're going to the cinema together.
Kevin	Can't you see him another time?
Sarah	No – he's far too important. He's got a flash car and everything!

Sarah exits stage-left while the Professor enters from stage-right.

Professor	*(Rubbing his hands in excitement)* Well, Kevin. What time are they arriving?
Kevin	*(Shuffling awkwardly and looking at his feet)* Um. They're not.
Professor	*(Taken aback)* What? They must be!
Kevin	They're sort of busy. They did say sorry.
Professor	What good is that? I've bought the food now. And the drink. Someone's got to have it!
Kevin	*(Rubbing his stomach)* I will.
Professor	*(Ignoring Kevin's comment)* I know, Kevin! Go out and invite all the poor people – the sick and the homeless – the unemployed, the handicapped and the elderly. Tell them they can come to the party.
Kevin	*(Reluctantly)* Okay. If you insist!

Kevin exits stage-right. The Professor moves to the front of the audience.

Professor	*(Shrugs)* Tsk! I don't know! If my friends had come to the party, they could have had eternal life. They could go to the cinema whenever they liked. They could play video

15

games for eternity. They could even listen to Simply
Red records for ever and ever!
(Shakes his head)

*At this point Kevin returns with a group of people. They are in a very
sorry state. They shuffle across the stage – limping and coughing.*

Derek   Thank you for your invitation, sir.

Jean   We wouldn't miss this party for the world!

Professor *(Offering glass of serum)*
              Here – drink this!

They drink the serum and immediately begin to recuperate.

Derek   *(Stretching his arms)*
              Amazing! I feel ten years younger!

Jean   *(Jumping up and down)*
              Wow! This is brilliant!

Derek   *(To Professor)*
              How can we ever thank you?

Professor *(Shaking his head)*
              No need. Enjoy the party!

Jean   Can we bring our friends along?

Professor *(Nodding)*
              Of course! The more the merrier. If anyone wants
              eternal life, all they have to do is come and ask. It's here
              for the taking.

Derek   Come on, Jean – let's go and tell the others!

The group exit stage-right.

Professor Good work, Kevin. But there's still plenty of space. Go
              and invite even more people! As many as you can. I want
              you to cover the length and breadth of the city!

Kevin   But what about your friends, Professor? Shall I try
              again?

Professor *(Shaking his head)*
              No, Kevin – it's too late now. They had their chance and
              they turned it down. They can never come to my party.

Kevin   But they'll die, Professor!

Professor   *(Putting arm around Kevin's shoulder)*
I tried, Kevin. I really tried. But at the end of the day,
it was their choice . . .

Nearly Ready

All of us make excuses for not spending more time with God. We're too busy to pray, too tired to go to Church, too preoccupied to read the Bible. This sketch attempts to bring home the absurdity of our actions. Rather than taking time to talk with the creator of the universe – the saviour of mankind – we'd rather watch 'Blind Date'. Trivial matters distract us from the most important one of all.

Cast   Sue
Jesus

Props   Chair
Items of furniture
Glass
Jumper
Toothbrush

Sue is sitting on a single chair centre-stage. She is bored – gazing around, looking at her watch, and twiddling her thumbs. She yawns and stretches her arms. After thirty seconds or so, Jesus appears stage-right and mimes knocking on the dooor.

Jesus   Hello? Hello? Are you there, Sue?

Sue   *(Bored)*
Who is it?

Jesus   It's me – Jesus!

Sue   *(Jumping out of her seat and panicking)*
Jesus?!

Jesus   Yes. Can I come in, please?

Sue   *(Rushing around)*
Er . . . what for?

Jesus   I'd like to say hello.

Sue   *(Trying to hide under her chair)*
Right . . . um . . . I'll be right with you . . .

Jesus   Okay.

Still under the chair, Sue creeps towards the door. At the last minute she stops.

Sue   Hang on! I just need to tidy up. Won't be a minute!

Jesus   If you say so.

Sue climbs out from underneath the chair and runs around the place rearranging furniture – moving stuff only to put it back again. She turns the chair on its side, upside down, and back to front. Jesus waits at the door, looking at his watch, before knocking again.

Jesus   Sue? Are you ready yet?

Sue   *(Frozen to the spot)*
               Yup! Ready!

Jesus   Can you let me in then?

Sue   Er . . . okay!
               (Walks towards the door and then stops)
               Hang on! I'm just going to get changed!

Jesus   What for?

Sue   Um . . . I've just spilt some water . . .

Jesus   Where?

Sue   *(Picks up glass of water and pours it over her jumper)*
               On my jumper!

Jesus   Well, hurry up, will you? I'm getting bored out here.

Sue puts on a different jumper.

Sue   Okay. All done! Ready!

Jesus   Great.
               (Knocking on the door)
               Open the door, will you?

Sue   Right! Straight away!
               (Hesitating)
               Hold it! I've just remembered! I'd better brush my teeth.

Jesus   What for?

Sue   To stop tooth decay!
               (Starts brushing her teeth)

Jesus   Can't you do that later?

Sue   *(Mouthful of toothbrush)*
               Nearly ready!

Jesus   *(Knocking on door)*
               You're not trying to avoid me, are you, Sue?

19

Sue   *(Exaggerating)*
              Avoid you? Huh! Don't be ridiculous! I'll be right with
              you . . .

Jesus   Okay!

Sue   *(Pause)*
              I'll just finish watching TV.

Jesus   What?!

Sue mimes turning on a TV set. She sits on the chair and watches the screen.

Jesus   *(Knocking on the door)*
              Sue! Please open the door!

Sue   *(Sighing and walking slowly to the door)*
              Alright, alright. Keep your hair on!

Sue pauses by the door, draws a deep breath, and opens the door. Immediately she feigns a huge smile.

Sue   *(Shaking him roughly by the hand and slapping him heartily on the back)*
              Hi, Jesus! Great to see you!

Jesus   Nice to see you, Sue. Can I come in now?

Sue   Ah!
              (Looking around embarrassed)
              Tell you what – could you come back tomorrow? I mean
              (Pause)
              – it's nothing particularly urgent, is it?

Give and Take

This is a very short sketch which gets straight to the point. Jesus offers us the greatest gifts imaginable. All he asks in return is commitment. Sadly, apathy and ingratitude always get the better of us.

Cast   Simon
            Jesus

Props Table
            Two chairs

Jesus and Simon are sitting at a table facing each other.

Simon   Okay, Jesus. I propose we make a deal.

Jesus   *(Nodding)*
            Okay. Let's hear it.

Simon   For you, I am prepared to go to church now and again. Not too often, mind: just enough to keep my conscience clean . . . I'll read my Bible every once in a while, and I'll pray – but only when I'm in trouble.

Jesus   Go on.

Simon   I'll follow the Ten Commandments.
            (Pause)
            Well, most of them . . . I mean, I haven't killed anyone . . . and the one about 'Taking the Lord's name in vain' doesn't really count anymore, does it?
            (Pause)
            As for 'Do not lie' . . . Well, in this day and age you've got to, haven't you?
            (He pauses and looks at Jesus.)

Jesus   *(Shaking his head)*
            No, not really.

Simon   I'll love my neighbour – if he loves me. I won't succumb to temptation – unless I have to . . . but if anyone asks, I'll deny all knowledge of you.
            (Pause)
            How's that?

Jesus   *(Nodding)*
Okay. Here's *my* proposition. For you, I'll come to earth as a human being . . . suffer ridicule, humiliation, and poverty . . . undergo unfair trial, be persecuted, rejected by my friends, and betrayed. Eventually I'll be whipped, spat upon, and killed in a barbaric execution . . . Then I'll return to life, only to be rejected again and again.
(Pause)
What do you think? Is that a good deal or what?

Simon   *(Long pause)*
Hmm . . . I'll think about it . . .

They both freeze, staring at each other.

Heaven's Gate

It's a common misconception that 'Nice People' are guaranteed a place in the Kingdom of Heaven. Live a decent life, give regularly to charity, feed stray cats, and you're in. But the Bible tells us only through faith in Jesus Christ can we be sure of eternal life (John 14.6). Salvation depends on commitment to Christ rather than our own merits.

Cast St Peter
St Anne
Roger Perkins
Georgia

Props Curriculum Vitae
Book

St Peter and St Anne stand centre-stage dressed all in white. Perkins enters from stage-right. He is dressed in his best suit and tie. From his speech and manner he appears very self-confident.

Perkins Hello. Is this the kingdom of God?

St Anne That's right. Entrance is just over there.
(Points stage-left)

Perkins Marvellous.
(Shaking both by the hand)
How do you do? The name's Perkins. Roger Perkins.

St Peter How do you do, Mr Perkins. I'm St Peter and this is St Anne.

St Anne *(Nodding)*
Hello.

St Peter How can we help you?

Perkins Well, I wonder if I can enter Heaven?

St Anne *(Sceptical)*
You want to enter the kingdom of God?

Perkins Yes. I hope that's alright. I've always wanted to go to Heaven. Well, ever since dying anyway . . . The moment I saw it I thought,
(Spreads arms)
'That's the place for me.'

23

St Peter	*(Scratching chin)* Hmm . . . In that case you'll have to pass the entrance requirements.
Perkins	No problem. *(Removes piece of paper from pocket)* I've brought a copy of my CV. You'll find all my life details there. *(Offers it to St Anne)*
St Anne	No need, Mr Perkins. *(Rips up the piece of paper)* I've already got a copy. *(Holds up large book. On the paper dust jacket the word 'Perkins' is written in big capital letters.)* The unedited version.
St Peter	We'll just need to ask you a number of questions. Are you ready?
Perkins	Oh yes. *(Rubbing his hands)* Is it like 'Trivial Pursuit'? I'm good at that. Especially sport.
St Anne	*(Consulting the book)* Right then . . . Number one.
Perkins	*(Folds arms and waits)* Ready when you are!
St Anne	Have you led a Christian life?
Perkins	*(Taken aback and disappointed)* Um . . . Sort of . . . I went to church now and again. Weddings, Christenings, that kind of thing . . .
St Peter	Go on.
Perkins	*(Flushed)* And I've never killed anyone – or committed adultery . . . Well, not much anyway.

St Peter and St Anne look at each other and frown.

St Anne	*(Consulting book)* Number two. Who is the Son of God?
Perkins	*(Cheering up)* Ah yes! I know this one! Moses!

St Peter and St Anne sigh.

St Peter Wrong.

Perkins *(Tentatively)*
Abraham?

St Anne Wrong.

Perkins *(Panicking)*
David?

St Peter *(Bored)*
Wrong.

Perkins *(Desperate)*
The Archbishop of Canterbury?

St Anne *(Shaking her head)*
Not who I had in mind, no.

St Peter Number three. Who died for your sins?

Perkins *(Scratching his head)*
Er . . . Pass.
(Pause)
Can I have a sport one now?

St Anne *(Ignoring him and consulting book)*
Number four. Have you forgiven those who sinned against you?

Perkins *(Taken aback)*
You must be joking!

St Peter Well, I'm afraid to say . . .

Perkins *(Interrupting)*
Hang on! I know a Bible verse – surely that counts?
(Thinking)
Now . . . let's see . . . Oh yes! 'I am the way, the truth, and the life'.

St Anne *(Encouraged)*
And what does that mean, Mr Perkins?

Perkins *(Shrugging)*
Don't have a clue, I'm afraid.

St Peter and St Anne groan.

Georgia enters from stage-right wearing T-shirt, jeans, and trainers.

Georgia   *(Nervously)*
Excuse me – is this the kingdom of God?

Perkins   *(Sarcastic)*
No – it's Disneyworld.

St Peter   *(Ignoring him)*
How can we help you?

Georgia   I wonder if I could come in?

Perkins   *(To audience)*
Oh dear. She doesn't stand a chance! She's not even wearing a jacket!

Perkins folds his arms and watches cynically.

St Peter   We'll just have to ask you some questions.

Georgia   Okay.

St Anne   *(Consulting book)*
Number one. Have you led a Christian life?

Georgia   Well, I've always tried to.

St Peter   Number two. Who is the Son of God?

Georgia   I believe the Son of God is Jesus Christ.

St Anne   *(Consulting book)*
Number three. Who died for your sins?

Georgia   Jesus. He died for my sins when he was crucified.

St Peter   Number four. Have you forgiven those who sinned against you?

Georgia   *(Nodding)*
Yes, I have. It wasn't easy. But I have.

Perkins   *(Laughing)*
Tsk! That was hopeless!

St Anne   Congratulations, Madam. You are free to enter!

Georgia   *(Excited)*
Great!
(She hurries off stage-left)

Perkins	*(Outraged)* You what?!
St Peter	*(Concerned)* Is something the matter, Mr Perkins?
Perkins	*(Shaking his fist)* You bet there is! That's not fair!
St Anne	Why not?
Perkins	I was here before her!
St Peter	But she put her faith in Jesus. She can come in.
Perkins	*(Getting increasingly desperate)* Look – please let me in . . . I'm pretty good on the harp . . . I love singing hymns – especially 'Kum ba Yah'. *(Gets down on his knees)* And I bought a Cliff Richard album once!
St Anne	*(Shaking her head)* I'm very sorry, Mr Perkins – but we can't help you. If you don't believe that Jesus died for your sins, then you're not forgiven. And if you're not forgiven, you can't enter Heaven.
Perkins	*(Standing up and dejected)* So what's going to happen to me?
St Peter	I'm afraid we've got no alternative but to send you downstairs . . .

St Peter and St Anne exit stage-left. Perkins looks extremely downcast. He sighs.

Perkins	I knew I should have worn my blue tie!

Easter Eggs and Easter Errors

It's a common complaint that the true meaning of Christmas has been forgotten. But the meaning of Easter is even more neglected. Most people associate Easter with chocolate, eggs and queues on the M4. It's a glorious celebration that's been stolen by big business. Let's steal it back.

Cast Monica Wright
Reverend Donkin
Andrew

Props Desk
Telephone

Monica stands centre-stage talking on the telephone. She is dressed smartly.

Monica Alright, Kevin – that's thirty thousand caramel centres, forty thousand cream centres, and twenty thousand plain. Got that?
(Pause)
Okay – fax me an estimate by 9 am tomorrow. Got it?
(Puts down phone)

Andrew, Monica's secretary, enters.

Andrew Ms Wright?

Monica *(Snapping)*
Yes? What is it, Andrew?

Andrew The Reverend Donkin is here to see you.

Monica Right. Send him in.

Andrew Whatever you say.
(Looks off-stage and waves Donkin on)
Ms Wright will see you now, Reverend.

Donkin *(Entering)*
Jolly good.

Monica *(Giving Donkin a very powerful handshake)*
Reverend Donkin, great to see you! Thanks for popping in.

Donkin My pleasure, Miss . . . er . . . ?

Monica *(Another gripping handshake)*
Wright. Monica Wright, President of Ruddberry's Chocolate. We need your help, Vicar – and we need it bad.

Donkin	What would you like? Hymn singing? Prayer meetings? Coffee mornings?
Monica	*(Shaking her head)* No -- we need some help with our new Easter campaign.
Donkin	*(Confused)* Easter campaign?
Monica	We're launching some new chocolate eggs.
Donkin	*(More confused)* Chocolate eggs?!
Monica	We're planning to saturate the impulse market.
Donkin	*(Utterly confused)* Impulse market?!!
Monica	*(Annoyed)* Look, what are you – a vicar or an echo?
Donkin	I'm very sorry, Ms Wright, but I don't see why you need a vicar to saturate the impulse market.
Monica	Simple. We're going to get back to basics. Start again. Stress the true spirit of Easter.
Donkin	You mean the Christian spirit?
Monica	Exactly! And what we need from you are some Bible verses. Got it?
Donkin	Got it! *(Keen)* What would you like?
Monica	*(Dramatically)* Something on Easter eggs!
Donkin	Ah! *(Shuffles uncomfortably and coughs)* Tricky . . .
Monica	What's the problem?
Donkin	Um . . . There aren't any.
Monica	*(Disappointed)* Oh dear.

	(Pause while she scratches her head and thinks) Alright – how about something on daffodils?
Donkin	*(Shaking his head)* Nothing, I'm afraid.
Monica	Are you sure?
Donkin	*(Nodding)* Positive. There is nothing in the Bible about daffodils.
Monica	*(Sighs)* That's a shame . . . *(Scratches her head)* What about Easter bonnets?
Donkin	*(Shaking head)* Nope.
Monica	Bunny rabbits?
Donkin	*(Shaking head)* Nope.
Monica	The James Bond film on TV?
Donkin	*(Shaking head)* Not a sausage, I'm afraid.
Monica	*(Pacing up and down)* Look – how can Easter be a Christian festival if there's nothing in the Bible about chocolate eggs, daffodils, bonnets, bunny rabbits, or the James Bond film on TV?!!
Donkin	*(Slowly and with emphasis)* Because Easter is about Jesus.
Monica	*(Confused)* What are you talking about?
Donkin	We celebrate Easter because the Son of God overcame death. He died on a cross so that we could be made perfect, and spend eternal life with him in Heaven.
Monica	So where do the chocolate eggs come in?
Donkin	I'm afraid they don't. They've become something of a red herring.
Monica	So, basically, Easter is about a man dying on a cross to give us eternal life?

Donkin   *(Nodding)*
          Exactly.

Monica   *(Overjoyed)*
          Reverend Donkin – that is amazing!
          (Yet another firm handshake)
          That is the most incredible, exciting, and challenging
          thing I've ever heard!

Donkin   I know. It's hard to believe, isn't it?

Monica   Just wait till I tell the others. This is going to be huge!
          (Grabbing him by the shoulders)
          Reverend Donkin – how can I get involved?

Donkin   You mean you want to become a Christian?

Monica   No – I want to make a Son of God chocolate bar! Just
          imagine the publicity . . . We'll sell millions!

Monica exits excitedly. Donkin groans and holds his head in his hands.

The First Church

An editor, not wholly unconnected with this publication, pointed out that most Christian drama is based around events in the Old Testament or parables. Why aren't there any sketches based on New Testament events? Rising to the challenge, I rapidly realised why. New Testament sketches are really hard to write.

Eventually this sketch came together – a comparison between the church the Apostles built in the early first century, and that two thousand years later. It stresses the need for the church to concentrate on Christ, and not the politics and logistics that surround it.

Cast   Peter
Luke
Mary
Martha
John

Props   Biblical head-dresses
Five chairs

Five people sit in a semi-circle. In the centre is Peter.

Peter   Well, everybody. What a couple of weeks, eh?

Everyone nods and murmurs in agreement.

Peter   First Jesus dies on the cross, then he comes back from the dead, and then he ascends to Heaven in a blaze of glory!
(Pause)
Talk about strange!

Everyone nods and murmurs some more.

Luke   The question is, Peter: as disciples, what do we do now?

Yet more nodding and murmuring.

Peter   Well, I thought we could form a church.

Mary   *(Confused)*
A what?

Peter   A church. A group of people getting together on a regular basis to study the Bible, pray, break bread, and enjoy fellowship.

Everyone looks at Peter blankly.

Peter	*(Looking around)* Something wrong?
Martha	Not really . . . It's just I thought a church was somewhere you went to show off your best clothes . . .
Peter	*(Shaking his head)* No, Martha – you can wear whatever you like. God doesn't mind. He looks at the inside – not the outside. Okay?

Everyone reluctantly agrees.

Peter	Right – let's move on.
John	*(Raising his hand)* Um . . . Peter?
Peter	Yes?
John	Isn't a church somewhere you have lots of coffee mornings? Where you sit around and gossip about people?
Peter	*(Shaking his head)* No, John – that's a Staff Room. Coffee after a meeting is all well and good, but it's the meeting before that's important.
Luke	What about the gossip?
Peter	*(Firmly)* A church doesn't gossip, Luke.
Luke	What – never?
Peter	Never. Okay?

Everyone reluctantly agrees.

Peter	Now, I thought our church could meet every Sunday . . .
Mary	*(Raising her hand)* Um . . . Peter?
Peter	*(Slightly irritated)* Yes?
Mary	When we go to church, are we going to sing lots of boring hymns?
Martha	With no tune . . . ?

John   And two hundred and seventy eight verses . . . ?

Peter   *(Shaking his head)*
Look – there's more to church than singing hymns. Much more.
(Pause)
Besides, not all hymns are boring. Okay?

Everyone reluctantly agrees.

Peter   Now, if we meet during the week for Bible study . . .

Martha   *(Raising her hand)*
Um . . . Peter?

Peter   *(Irritated)*
Yes?

Martha   Isn't church somewhere people go to ease their conscience?

Peter   *(Shaking his head)*
It's not an act, Martha. Church is somewhere people go to worship God. They spend time with him, they talk to him, and they listen to him. It's not about pretending and it's not about guilt. People go to church because they want to. Okay?

Everyone reluctantly agrees.

Peter   Right, let's crack on . . .

Luke   *(Raising his hand)*
Um . . . Peter?

Peter   *(Plainly irritated)*
What is it now?

Luke   If we're going to form a church, to honour God and spread the good news about Jesus . . . ?

Peter   Yes?

Luke   Then I think we really need to sort out the big issues.

Peter   Good idea, Luke. Like teaching people about Jesus and helping them to live as Christians?

Luke   No – like who's going to deliver the parish magazine.

Peter   *(Disbelief)*
What?

Mary	*(Nodding)* And who's going to arrange the flower rota.
Peter	What are you talking about?
John	*(Raising his hand)* Don't forget choir practise!

Everyone nods in hearty agreement.

Peter	*(Shushing them)* Look – that is not what church is all about! Alright, alright – we need people to deliver the parish magazine, to arrange the flowers, and to hold choir practise . . . But the most important thing about church is Jesus. Learning how to love him and how to live for him.

They all look at him blankly.

Peter	Okay?

Everyone mumbles in reluctant agreement.

Luke	Alright, Peter – we'll form a church.
Peter	Good.
Mary	But on one condition . . .
Peter	What's that?
Mary	We can criticize the sermon over Sunday lunch.

Everyone nods in agreement. Peter groans.

Holiday Camp

This sketch is for use at Christian residential camps – or to promote them during a church service. The references to 'Pathfinder camp' is arbitrary and can be replaced by the name of any kind of camp. Similarly the names given to Tarquin's friends can also be replaced with real ones. The more relevant to the actual camp, the better.

Tarquin's experiences stress that a relationship with Jesus can be just as exciting and meaningful as a relationship with a contemporary – indeed more so. The sketch also tackles many of the popular misconceptions about Christians and Christian behaviour.

Cast   Tarquin
Mother
Father

Props   Pipe
Magazine
Suitcase
Three chairs
Cushions
Hankie

Mother and Father are sitting on stage. They look rather posh and snobby. The Father is dressed in a suit and puffing on a pipe. The Mother wears plenty of expensive jewellery and is flicking through a copy of a smart magazine e.g. 'Horse and Hound'. Tarquin enters lugging an enormous suitcase. He looks completely normal – wearing jeans, trainers, and baseball cap.

Tarquin   Hello, everybody – I'm back!

Mother and Father stand up. Father pats him on the back and takes his case. Mother embraces him.

Mother   Tarquin! You're home! Come to Mumsie!

Father   We missed you, son. Bally good to see you!

Tarquin   *(Struggling free of Mother's embrace)*
I missed you too, Mum and Dad. Respect due!

Father pulls puzzled expression.

Mother   So did you enjoy (Pathfinder) camp?

Tarquin   Oh yeah! It was well wicked!

Father   *(Even more puzzled)*
Wicked?

Tarquin   You know – fun.

Mother   Oh. How lovely, darling. And did you make any nice friends?

Tarquin   Oh yeah – loads!

Father   Really? How absolutely super! Who are they?

Tarquin   There was Mark, Jim, Rachel, Emma, Jesus –

Mother   Jesus?! That's rather an unusual name . . .

Father   It's not Jesus Fortescue-Jones, is it?

Tarquin   No, Dad.
(Slowly and patiently)
Jesus Christ.

Mother   Well, I've never met anyone called Jesus before.
(Pause)
Is he Welsh?

Tarquin   *(Confused)*
Er, no – he was born in Bethlehem, actually.

Father   You mean he's foreign?!
(Disappointed)
Oh, Tarquin – how could you?

Tarquin   You should meet him. He's a really great bloke.

Mother   *(Putting her arm around him)*
But, Tarquin, my precious – we didn't send you to camp to meet funny Welsh people. We wanted you to enjoy yourself.

Tarquin   But I did! It was fantastic.

Father   Well, sit down and tell us all about it, there's a good chap!

Mother fusses with the cushions on Tarquin's chair. Eventually they all sit down.

Mother   Go on then – tell us what you did.

Tarquin   Well, we played football, went hiking, had midnight feasts . . .

Father   *(Nodding in approval)*
That's more like it . . . Jolly good.

Tarquin	We went swimming, played on the beach . . .
Mother	*(Clasping her hands)* Oh, how marvellous.
Tarquin	And we had brilliant prayer meetings.
Mother & Father	*(Jumping out of their seats with a look of horror)* You what?!
Tarquin	We had prayer meetings. We'd sit around together and pray.
Mother	*(Putting hands to head and over-reacting)* What have we done, Geoffrey? We've turned our child into a Hare Krishna!
Tarquin	Don't be silly, Mum – I'm not a Hare Krishna.
Father	*(Wiping his brow)* Phew! Thank heavens for that!

Mother and Father sit down again.

Tarquin	No – I'm a Christian.
Mother & Father	*(Jumping up again with even more horror)* You what?!
Tarquin	I'm a Christian. I've started reading the Bible and everything.
Mother	*(Folding her arms)* You'll be shaving your hair off next. And wearing sandals.
Tarquin	No, I won't! Christians are just like everyone else. They wear jeans, listen to pop music, and they like hamburgers.
Father	Jesus Fortescue-Jones doesn't like hamburgers . . .
Tarquin	*(Shrugging)* I don't care. *(Pointing at himself)* I'm completely normal.
Mother	I bet this lad Jesus Christ has got something to do with it!
Father	*(Shaking fist)* Wait till I meet his parents!

Tarquin	I'm not sure you'll be able to, Dad.
Father	What are you talking about?
Tarquin	Well, his Dad was never actually on the earth, and his Mum died two thousand years ago. In fact, Jesus died two thousand years ago. But only for three days.
Mother	*(Taking him by the scruff of the neck)* Tarquin – have you been taking drugs?
Tarquin	No.
Father	*(Peering at him)* You haven't been drinking, have you?
Tarquin	Only Pepsi Max.
Mother	There's only one explanation then. *(Throws hands in the air)* He's gone mad! *(Starts sobbing. Dabs her eyes with a hankie)*
Father	Mad as a hatter, if you ask me.
Mother	*(Swivelling a finger at her temple)* His mind's turned to putty.
Father	The lights are on, the door's open – but . . . *(Tapping his temple)* . . . Mr Brain's not at home.
Tarquin	There is one other explanation, actually.
Mother	*(Doubtful but soppy)* And what's that, honeybun?
Tarquin	I'm telling the truth. Jesus is alive – because he's the Son of God. He's overcome death – and now he's Prince of Peace, King of kings . . . *(Pause)* . . . and my mate.
Father	*(Cheering up)* What was that?
Mother	*(Curious)* He's a prince?
Father	*(Excited)* King of kings?

Tarquin	*(Nodding)* And my mate.
Mother	Well, if he's Royalty that's an entirely different matter.
Father	Yes. You must invite him round to tea at once, Tarquin.
Mother	*(Cuddling him)* Mmmm. I'll make some scones.
Father	*(Clutching Mother's arm)* See, Daphne. I knew sending him to (Pathfinder) camp was a good idea!

Good News

I wish I could say this sketch was based on my own experience. Unfortunately not once have I been whisked off to Barbados, been offered a salary of £18,000, or won the pools. Fortunately I have been offered eternal life, forgiveness, and intimate friendship with the creator of the entire universe. And I know which I'd rather have.

The sketch emphasises the ridiculous twisted values we hold. We hanker for transient pleasures, and ignore those which last forever. I wish I knew why.

Cast   June
          Mr Lewis
          Ian
          Jesus

Props   Mug
          Envelope
          Giant cheque

June enters carrying a coffee mug and rubbing her eyes. She's obviously just got up. Her clothes are scruffy and clumsily buttoned etc. A large envelope is lying on the floor downstage.

June   Oh well. Another day – another cup of coffee . . .
               (Looks at watch)
               Twenty past eight . . .
               (Sighs)
               Late again!
               (Walks downstage and picks up envelope)
               Oh! A letter!
               (Frowns)
               Probably another bill . . .
               (Opens envelope and reads)
               'Dear Miss Simpson, I am delighted to tell you that you have won first prize in our competition. You have won a free holiday to Barbados for three weeks . . . '
               (Throwing envelope into the air delighted)
               Wha-hey! I'm going to Barbados! For three weeks! I can't believe it! Wait till I tell everybody . . .
               (Carries on muttering excitedly)

As June rabbits on, Mr Lewis appears stage-right dressed extremely smartly. He mimes picking up a phone and dialling a number. He makes the ringing noise.

June   Crikey! The phone!
                (Rushes stage-left and mimes picking up a phone)
                Hello?

Lewis   Hello, Miss Simpson?

June   Speaking.

Lewis   This is Brendan Lewis of Lewis, Lewis and Thwaite. I'm ringing about your job application.

June   *(Nervous)*
                Oh right. I hope you like it.

Lewis   Like it? We love it! Congratulations! You've got the job.

June   *(Delighted)*
                Oh wow! That's amazing!

Lewis   Your starting salary will be £18,000. I hope that's alright.

June   *(Disbelief)*
                £18,000?!! But that's loads!

Lewis   And you'll get eight weeks holiday per year. Is that okay?

June   That's fantastic! Thanks very much.

Lewis   Super. See you Monday morning then? Goodbye!

June   Goodbye!

They both mime putting down the telephone. Mr Lewis exits.

June   *(Pacing about excitedly)*
                I can't believe this! Free holiday in Barbados and a new job. This is incredible!

Ian enters stage-left and mimes pressing a doorbell. He impersonates the ring.

June   That's the door. Now what?
                (Crosses stage-left and mimes opening the door)
                Hello?

Ian   Hello. Miss Simpson?

June   Yes?

Ian	Miss June Simpson?
June	That's right.
Ian	I'm from Littlewoods. You've won the Pools.
June	*(Shocked)* What?!
Ian	You've just won three billion trillion zillion pounds. Do you want cash or a cheque?
June	*(Bewildered)* Um . . . Cheque, I suppose . . .
Ian	Okay. *(Handing over a huge cheque covered with noughts)* There you go!
June	*(Struggling with the cheque)* Thanks very much . . . Goodbye!

June mimes closing the door as Ian exits.

June	This is brilliant! Free holiday, new job, and three billion trillion zillion pounds! Talk about good news!

Another man appears at the door, dressed plainly. He rings the doorbell.

June	*(Rubbing her hands together)* That's probably Tom Cruise asking to marry me. Or the Queen with an OBE. Or U2 looking for a new singer.

The man rings the bell again, so June crosses the stage and opens the door.

June	Hello?
Jesus	Hello. June Simpson?
June	Yes?
Jesus	June Valerie Simpson – Number Two Pine Close?
June	That's right. How can I help you?
Jesus	My name's Jesus. I've got some good news for you. In fact, it's the best news ever.
June	*(Hooked)* Really? Go on!

Jesus   I'm here to offer you eternal life, forgiveness, and intimate friendship with the creator of the entire universe.

June   *(Disappointed)*
              Oh.
              (Pause)
              Is that it?

Jesus   Oh no – that's just the start! I'll give you true happiness, inner peace, and undying love – for eternity!

June   *(Looking at him blankly)*
              No marriage proposal then?

Jesus   *(Surprised at the suggestion)*
              Not as such.

June   No OBE?

Jesus   Not really.

June   No best-selling albums?

Jesus   Nope – just love, peace, and happiness!

June   *(Sighs)*
              Not today, thank you. Goodbye!

As Jesus tries to interrupt, June slams the door on his face. As he continues to wait, she collects her cheque and shuffles centre-stage.

June   *(Shrugs)*
              Tsk! And I thought this was my lucky day . . .

She exits. Jesus hangs his head in disappointment and freezes.

The Shepherds' Christmas

This is a reminder of the true meaning of Christmas – all too easily forgotten in this day and age.

Cast   Ben
Joshua
Lydia
Ruth

Props   Sheep
Gift-wrapped ties (preferably in large boxes)

Four shepherds sit around the stage. One or two toy sheep surround them. People off-stage can make the occasional sheep noise. A small pile of presents sit to one side.

Ben   *(Rubbing his hands to keep warm)*
Brr! It's cold tonight, ain't it, Lydia?

Lydia   *(Shivering)*
Freezing.

Joshua   *(Blowing on his hands)*
Sure is. But at least the sheep are warm.

Ruth   *(Huddled into a ball)*
I wish we had big woolly coats . . .

Ben   *(Looking into the distance)*
I bet it's warm in Bethlehem tonight.

Lydia   *(Following his gaze)*
It's very busy down there. All the hotels are full. I reckon you'd be lucky to get a one star stable!

Joshua   Still – at least Christmas is coming, eh?

They all cheer.

Ruth   What do you want for Christmas, Ben?

Ben   I could do with a new robe. With fur trimmings.

Lydia   I'd like a nice pair of thermal socks.

Joshua   I want a Super Nintendo.

Ruth   Joshua – you can't have a Super Nintendo!

Joshua   Why not?

Ben	It's Nought BC – they haven't been invented yet.
Joshua	Oh.
	(Slightly nonplussed then grumpily)
	Well, I wish they'd get a move on. I'm bored of playing 'I Spy'.
	(Getting more excited by the thought)
	I want to play 'Star Raiders' and 'Galactic Nightmare'.
	(Mimes playing a video game and imitates sound effects)
Lydia	What do you want for Christmas, Ruth?
Ruth	Um. I'd like God to come down to earth as a human being.
Ben	*(Scratching his head)*
	'Ere. I don't think they do those in the shops.
Joshua	You could try a mail order catalogue?
Lydia	That's no good.
Joshua	Why not?
Ruth	It's Nought BC – they haven't been invented yet.
Joshua	*(Disappointed)*
	Oh yeah.
Ben	You could ask Jeremiah's shepherds over there
	(Points to behind audience)
Lydia	I wouldn't bother, Ben. Jeremiah's shepherds are as thick as two short planks.

They nod their heads in agreement.

Ben	I reckon the sheep have got more brains than them.
Lydia	Jeremiah thought a sheep dip was a roller coaster ride . . .

They all laugh.

Ruth	I wonder if God will come as a shepherd . . .
Joshua	Ruth, why would God come to earth?
Ruth	Well, it's predicted in the Bible. Take Isaiah, for example.
Lydia	Isaiah Smith – the Bethlehem camel trader?
Ruth	No – Isaiah the Prophet. He said a child would be born and that he'd be called Emmanuel.
Joshua	Emmanuel? That's a funny name.

Ruth   It means 'God is with us'.

Ben   Look – call me old-fashioned, but if you ask me Christmas is all about turkey, decorations, and presents. It is not about a child called Emmanuel.

Lydia   Yeah, Ben's right. What good is a child at Christmas? Unless I get something wrapped up, covered with tinsel, or served with potatoes and gravy, I'm not interested.

Ruth   But Lydia, when this child grows up, he'll become a great leader. He'll overcome evil, death, and pain. And we'll have eternal life in heaven.

Joshua   *(Sitting up)*
             What was that? Eternal life?!

Ben   In Heaven?!

Lydia   Now that is a good Christmas present.

Ben   *(Nodding)*
             Better than a new robe.

Lydia   Much better than thermal socks.

Joshua   Much much better than a Super Nintendo.
             (Pause)
             Probably.

Ruth   *(Nodding)*
             Definitely better.

Joshua   So this present – how are you going to wrap it?

Ruth   Well, I guess somebody will deliver it. An angel or something.

Ben   An angel? In Bethlehem?! Fat chance!

Lydia   Yeah. You wouldn't catch an angel around here.

Joshua   An angel in Bethlehem is about as likely as three wise men following a star!

They nod their heads in agreement. Meanwhile, Ruth is busy looking into the distance, to a point behind the audience.

Ruth   Hang on. What's happening over there?

Ben   *(Peering)*
             It's Jeremiah's shepherds.

Lydia   *(Pointing)*
              There's a bright light in the sky!

Joshua   I can hear singing . . .

Ruth   And there's a strange star – over that stable.

Ben   *(Folding his arms)*
              Well, I'm sure there's a perfectly rational explanation . . .

Lydia   It's probably a firework display.

They nod their heads and mutter in agreement.

Joshua   With rockets and catherine wheels.

More nodding and noises of agreement.

Ben   And lasers!

Even more nodding and mumbles.

Ruth   Don't be stupid – it can't be!

Joshua   Why not?

Ruth   It's Nought BC – they haven't been invented yet!

All   Oh yeah.

They continue to peer into the back of the audience – speechless.

Lydia   *(Looking at her watch)*
              Hey! It's midnight. That means it's Christmas Day!

They all cheer.

Ben   Time for presents, everybody!

They cheer even louder. Excitedly they rush to the presents. Each simultaneously opens a packet containing a tie – preferably an exceptionally tasteless tie. Their disappointment is blatant.

Joshua   *(Groaning)*
              Oh no! A tie!

Ruth   I got a tie last year!

Lydia   And the year before . . .

Ben   And the year before that . . .

Joshua   *(Examining tie)*
              I don't suppose it's got a Super Nintendo inside . . . ?

Lydia   *(Shrugs)*
            Maybe next year, eh?

Everyone gives an enormous sigh and looks dejected. Ruth smiles.

Ben   *You're* not disappointed though, are you, Ruth?

Ruth   *(Shaking her head)*
           Not really, Ben. I reckon I got just what I wanted . . .

As the shepherds look down at their ties, Ruth looks into the distance and smiles.

The Christmas Feasibility Study

In a world in which advertisers and executives have hijacked Christmas, I thought it would be fun to turn the tables. Yet again, this is an attempt to illustrate the real reason for celebrating Christmas.

Cast   Anthony
            Belinda
            Crispin
            Danielle

Props   Flip-chart/Easel/Blackboard/OHP
            Christmas cards
            Picture of Father Christmas

Four smartly-dressed executives take the stage. They have a ridiculous drawl, swan around the stage and behave very pretentiously. They set up a flip-chart, easel, or blackboard. Anthony takes centre-stage. Where mentioned, the name of the advertising company (ABBZZNO & P) is spelt out and recited as quickly as possible.

Anthony   Good evening, ladies and gentlemen. My name's Anthony and I'm chief creative consultant for ABBZZNO & P Advertising. With me tonight I have my chief creative team.
(Points to each in turn)
Belinda.

Belinda   *(Waves)*
Hello.

Anthony   Crispin

Crispin   *(Flicks his hair)*
Hi.

Anthony   And Danielle.

Danielle   *(Adopts trendy pose)*
Yo! Respect to the local posse.

Anthony   As I'm sure you're aware, in recent times we've lost the true spirit of Christmas. People have got bored with the traditional festivities, and they've forgotten its true nature. Now as we all know, a real traditional Christmas is all about getting presents, watching television, and eating and drinking far too much. But we

at ABBZZNO & P Advertising have come up with some revolutionary new ideas for celebrating Christmas.
(Signalling to Belinda)
Belinda.

Anthony moves back and Belinda takes centre-stage.

Belinda   Thanks, Anthony. Now we're all familiar with Christmas cards.
(Holds up examples)
Brightly coloured pieces of cardboard, depicting snowmen, Christmas trees, and Victorian people skating on frozen ponds. But we've come up with the radical idea of putting religious pictures on the front.
(Holds up examples)
We've got three wise men, shepherds, angels, even Mary and Joseph. Pretty original, I'm sure you'll agree.

Danielle   Religious pictures on Christmas cards?! People are going to think you're mad!

Belinda   That's not all, Danielle. We thought people could write religious messages inside them. Even a simple 'God bless' would do.
(Pauses then signals to Crispin)
Crispin.

Belinda moves back and Crispin takes centre-stage.

Crispin   Thanks, Belinda. Now as we all know, Christmas morning is traditionally spent playing with presents, cooking turkey, and sitting in front of the TV watching Noel Edmonds. But we've come up with a new idea. It's called . . .
(Turning flip-chart / writing on blackboard)
'Going to Church.'

Anthony   *(Steps forward)*
Sorry for interrupting, Crispin. But what on earth is 'Church?' Is it a holiday resort?

Crispin   No, Anthony. Church is that large building very near your home where people go on Sundays.

Belinda   *(Holds up hand)*
I thought that was called 'Tesco's?'

51

Crispin Nope – Church is somewhere people go to worship by singing hymns and praying.

Anthony Crispin – it's new, it's exciting, it's dangerous!
(Slaps him on the back)
I like it!

Crispin Thanks, Anthony. Now what I propose is that instead of sitting around at home on Christmas Day, people go to Church and worship.

Belinda That's one heck of an idea, Crispin.

Crispin Thanks, Belinda. That way, we can think of other people and not just ourselves. And say thanks for all the great stuff that we've been given.
(Pauses then signals to Danielle)
Danielle.

Crispin moves back and Danielle takes centre-stage.

Danielle Thanks, Crispin. Now most people spend Christmas at home with their families. This makes Christmas a brilliant time – for arguing. Families argue over presents, sweets, television, who gets the comfy sofa, who's eaten too many satsumas, and so on and so forth. But what we've come up with is a new concept called . . .
(Turns flip-chart / writing on blackboard)
. . . 'Being Nice'. Instead of criticising people, you're friendly to them. Instead of being selfish, you're generous. And instead of worrying about what people will give you – try to think about what you can give them.

Crispin *(Raising hand)*
You mean giving is better than receiving?

Danielle *(Nodding)*
That's right, Crispin. I know it sounds crazy – but it works!
(Pauses then signals to Anthony)
Anthony.

Danielle moves back and Anthony returns to centre-stage.

Anthony Thanks, Danielle. Finally we come to our most radical and controversial idea. When we think of Christmas, I'm

sure we all think of one particular person. A person who stands for all that is kind and good. The man who gave us the very name 'Christmas'.
(Pause)
That's right.
(Holds up picture)
Father Christmas. He's a large happy fella with a red suit and big white beard. Every year he gives presents to well-behaved children. But we felt Father Christmas was getting on a bit, so we've come up with a replacement:
(Turns flip-chart / writing on blackboard)
God.

Belinda   Anthony – what's this God look like?

Anthony   Unfortunately no one actually knows. We're pretty sure he's got a beard though. And the thing about God is, he doesn't just give presents – he gives everything. Food, drink, friends, you name it – he gives it. He even gave his own son. And here's the amazing coincidence, right – his son, Jesus, was born at Christmas.

Danielle   Sounds perfect, Anthony.

Anthony   Completely perfect, Danielle. And if people were to think about Jesus at Christmas, maybe we'd all have a much better time.

Crispin   Jesus at Christmas?! You'll be asking us to pray next . . .

Anthony   So there we have it – the ABBZZNO & P Advertising ideas for a brand new type of Christmas.

Belinda   But what are we going to do about the old Christmas?

Crispin   What about arguing with the family?

Danielle   Watching TV all day?

Belinda   Eating and drinking too much?

Anthony   Simple, everybody. We'll move that to Easter!

Everybody nods in agreement.

What's It All About?

This sketch arose from a bizarre desire to merge 'Smith & Jones' with 'Waiting for Godot'. Throw in some snooker references, and this is what you get.

The delivery should imitate that of the Mel and Griff head-to-head. The recurring phrase 'What's it all about?' should be delivered in a very over-the-top Cockney drawl – 'Woss-Eeet-Awl-Abaht?'

The long pauses provide plenty of opportunity for pulling faces and puckering lips. Looking quizzical throughout would be a great advantage. Don't be afraid to leave the pauses – the slower this sketch builds, the better.

Cast   Kevin
             Andy

Props   Two chairs

Two blokes sit on straight-back chairs, facing the audience. They speak slowly and with plenty of pauses.

Kevin   Andy?

Andy   Yes, Kevin?

Kevin   I've been thinking, right.

Andy   Yes, Kevin?

Kevin   What's it all about?

Andy   How do you mean?

Kevin   You know – life.

Andy   Oh yeah – life.

Kevin   I mean – it's pointless, innit? You're born, you go to school, you get married, you grow old, and then you die.
             (Pause)
             What's it all about?

Andy   *(Shrugs)*
             Search me, Kevin.

They sit deep in thought for a few seconds.

Kevin   *(Pause)*
             Maybe it's about enjoying yourself.

Andy	How do you mean?
Kevin	You know – having fun, being with your mates, living life to the full.
Andy	Yeah – and playing snooker.
Kevin	*(Ignoring him)* Maybe the human race is here to be happy.
Andy	Yeah. *(Pause)* Are you happy, Kevin?
Kevin	Not really, Andy.
Andy	*(Pause)* Me neither.
Kevin	*(Pause)* Instead of just sitting here, doing nothing, we should do something about it.
Andy	You're right, Kevin. Let's do something about it.

They both nod but neither of them move. They sit looking around the place – still thinking.

Kevin	*(Pause)* Andy?
Andy	Yes, Kevin?
Kevin	What's it all about?
Andy	*(Shrugs)* Search me, Kevin.
Kevin	*(Pause)* Maybe it's all about progress.
Andy	How do you mean?
Kevin	You know – improving yourself. Getting answers. Making discoveries. Perfecting things.
Andy	What? Like snooker?
Kevin	*(Ignoring him)* Maybe we're all here to broaden our minds and to expand our understanding.
Andy	Yeah.

	(Pause) And to play snooker.
Kevin	*(Pause)* Instead of just sitting here, doing nothing, we should do something about it.
Andy	*(Nodding)* You're right, Kevin. Let's do something about it.

They both nod but neither of them move. They sit looking around the place – still thinking.

Kevin	*(Pause)* Andy?
Andy	Yes, Kevin?
Kevin	What's it all about?
Andy	*(Shrugs)* Search me, Kevin.
Kevin	*(Pause)* Maybe it's about survival.
Andy	How do you mean?
Kevin	You know – reproduction. Propagation of the species. An eternal circle of life and death.
Andy	Yeah. It's like – we have children. Then they have children. The grandchildren have children. The great grandchildren have children. The great-great-
Kevin	*(Interrupting)* I get the message, Andy.
Andy	*(Pause)* Basically, it's all about children, Kevin.
Kevin	*(Nodding)* Children, Andy.
Andy	*(Pause)* And snooker.
Kevin	*(Ignoring him)* Instead of just sitting here, doing nothing, we should do something about it.

Andy   *(Nodding)*
           You're right, Kevin. Let's do something about it.

They both nod but neither of them move. They sit looking around the place – still thinking.

Kevin   *(Pause)*
           Andy?

Andy   Yes, Kevin?

Kevin   What's it all about?

Andy   *(Shrugs)*
           Search me, Kevin.

Kevin   *(Pause)*
           Maybe it's about God.

Andy   How do you mean?

Kevin   Maybe there's a God out there, Andy. A God who's made us, who looks after us, and who's made plans for us.

Andy   *(Nodding)*
           Could be, Kevin.
           (Pause)
           Does he play snooker?

Kevin   *(Ignoring him)*
           Maybe he made us for a reason. Maybe life's not pointless after all. Maybe he knows the answer.

Andy   *(Pause)*
           Do you reckon it's got anything to do with snooker?

Kevin   *(Pause)*
           You know, Andy – if there is a God out there, we really should do something about it.

Andy   *(Nodding)*
           You're right, Kevin. We really should do something about it.

Kevin   *(Pause)*
           As soon as we can.

Andy   *(Nodding)*
           As soon as we can.

Kevin   *(Pause)*
           Before it's too late.

Andy   *(Nodding)*
           Before it's too late.

They sit still – looking around the place. Still thinking.

Andy   *(Pause)*
           Kevin?

Kevin   Yes, Andy?

Andy   *(Pause)*
           Fancy a game of snooker?

They freeze.

The Reluctant Evangelist

It's not easy talking to people about your faith. It's hard enough with your friends – let alone strangers. This sketch stresses we can't all be Billy Graham – but that we have a duty to witness. What's important is that we learn to be confident in the Gospel. We have a powerful message and we shouldn't be embarrassed to share it.

Cast Julie
Bill
Sam
Bus Stop
Bus Driver
Bus Passengers

Props Bus stop sign
Bible
Newspapers

Someone stands centre-stage

holding a sign saying 'Bus Stop'. Bill enters and stands by the bus stop. He is waiting for a lift. He patiently looks at his watch and around the venue. To the side of the stage Julie comes on, talking to Sam.

Julie I can't do it, Sam! I'm scared!

Sam Don't be silly, Julie. You've got nothing to be scared of. Get out there and spread the Word!

Julie What if they're Jewish? Or Islamic? Or Trendy?!

Sam It doesn't matter. You know what to do. So go and do it!

Julie Alright, alright! I'm going in!

Sam *(Thumbs up)*
All the best!

Julie crosses the stage very slowly, very nervously. Sam beckons her on – waving encouragement. Whenever Bill looks in Julie's direction, she pretends to be doing something: tying her laces, jogging on the spot, blowing her nose, admiring the architecture, etc. Eventually she arrives next to Bill. Sam exits.

Julie Um. Hello.

Bill Hello.

Julie	*(Looking around nervously before loudly clearing her throat)* Um. Excuse me?
Bill	Yes?
Julie	Are you a . . . er . . .
Bill	What?
Julie	Are you a . . . er . . . I mean, have you ever . . . um . . .
Bill	What?
Julie	Um. *(Pause)* Do you know when the next bus is?
Bill	*(Shaking head)* No idea. I'm waiting for a lift.
Julie	Oh right.

Julie looks around a bit more. Shuffles on the spot. She pulls out a copy of the Bible.

Julie	*(Coughs)* Excuse me?
Bill	Yes?
Julie	Have you ever read the B-B-B-B . . .
Bill	I'm sorry?
Julie	Have you ever read the B-B-B-B-Bus timetable?
Bill	*(Puzzled)* No.
Julie	*(Pause)* Me neither.
Bill	Right. *(Pause)* I thought you were going to say Bible.
Julie	*(Feigns laughter -- very poorly)* Bible? How funny! No. I wasn't going to say Bible. I was going to say bus timetable.
Bill	But you're holding a Bible, aren't you?

Julie   *(Shaking her head)*
Oh no, no, no, no, no. Not at all. Bible? No, no, no, no.

Bill   *(Pointing at Bible in her hands)*
So what's that then?

Julie   *(Looks at Bible, looks at Bill, looks at the Bible, then looks at Bill)*
Oh that?! That's . . . um . . . the new Jeffrey Archer novel. In hardback.

Bill   Oh, right.

Julie looks around a bit – embarrassed. Meanwhile Sam enters – sneaking on furtively. She's obviously trying to overhear Julie's progress. Eventually she sidles up to Julie.

Sam   How's it going?

Julie   Oh . . . um . . . Really well.

Sam   Yeah?

Julie   Oh yeah. Going great guns. Better get the baptism water ready!

Sam   Brilliant! I'll leave you to it then.
(Slaps Julie on the back and exits)

Julie   *(Disappointed)*
Right . . . Super.

Julie puts the Bible away. She adjusts her clothes, fiddles with her hair and clears her throat.

Julie   *(Confidently)*
Excuse me.

Bill   Yes. Now what?

Julie   *(Still confident)*
I was just thinking to myself, and I'd like to ask you a very important question.

Bill   Okay. What is it?

Julie   *(Confidence rapidly deteriorating into an incomprehensible mumble)*
Do you believe in flibberdibberbibberder?

Bill   I'm sorry?

Julie   *(Confident)*
I said – do you believe in . . .
(Mumbling incoherently)
. . . flibberdibberbibberder?

Bill   I don't have a clue what you're talking about.

Julie   *(Shrugs)*
Oh well. Not to worry. I'll just wait for the bus.

Bill gives her a quizzical look before resuming his wait. At this point the bus enters. It is mimed by one person moving across the stage pretending to drive. Behind him a group of passengers shuffle along, pretending to be holding ceiling straps and making a slight rocking motion. One or two people are reading newspapers. The bus stops at the bus stop – much to Julie's embarrassment.

Driver   Number forty three, love?

Julie   Um. No, thanks.

Bill   I thought you were waiting for a bus?

Julie   Well, I think I'll wait for the next one. This one's not red enough.

Driver   Suit yourself.

The bus moves away and off-stage. While Bill is looking the other way, Julie pulls out her Bible and mimes a Billy Graham, Bible-thumping pose – wagging her finger and mouthing words. When Bill turns round suddenly she pretends to be reading.

Bill   Excuse me.

Julie   Yes?

Bill   Are you a Christian?

Julie   *(Looking at watch – feigning horror)*
Golly! Is that the time?! Well, I'd better get going. Nice meeting you. All the best!
(She starts walking off)

Bill   I thought you were waiting for a bus?

Julie   *(Stops)*
Um. Yes . . . I thought I'd wait for it over there . . .
(Points off-stage)

Bill	So are you a Christian or what?
Julie	*(Looks around nervously)* Um. Sort of.
Bill	So why don't you invite me to church?
Julie	Um. I thought you might . . . *(Shrugs)* You know.
Bill	Well, go on then. Invite me to church.
Julie	*(Surprised)* Oh. Okay then. *(Mumbling, looking at the ground)* Would you like to come to church?
Bill	*(Nodding)* Yes, please.
Julie	*(Dejected and gloomy)* See – I knew you wouldn't be interested!
Bill	I am!
Julie	*(Not listening)* Not to worry. Some other time maybe . . .
Bill	But I said yes!
Julie	*(Sullen)* I'll just go home. Forget I ever asked you.
Bill	Look – I would like to go to church. I'm really interested. I'm not a Christian but I'm keen to find out more. Please tell me about Jesus.
Julie	*(Disbelief)* What? You'd like to hear about Jesus?
Bill	*(Exasperated)* Yes!
Julie	Tsk! Why didn't you say so in the first place?! Tut! Are you scared or something?
Bill groans.	
Julie	*(Folding her arms)* Honestly! You only had to ask!

The Alternative Ten Commandments

Consider this piece a variation on 'The Screwtape Letters' – only not as good. The Ten Commandments are too easily overlooked in today's society. This sketch emphasises their relevance by showing how often they're broken and why. It also draws attention to the fact that evil does exist and is actively seeking to disrupt God's creation. Although the devils are figures of ridicule, they also need to be somewhat sinister – presenting a genuine threat.

Depending on the age group, the director might prefer to omit one or two lines. Please feel free to edit the sketch to your satisfaction.

Cast   Satan
Beelzebub
Scaramouche
Barry
(Although Satan and Barry need to be male parts, Beelzebub and Scaramouche can be female roles.)

Props   Four chairs
Pen
Clipboard

All four characters are sitting on stage. They are dressed in red and black. Satan is clutching a pen and a clipboard. The devils all speak with an evil accent – with wicked grins and evil chuckles.

Satan	*(Coughs)* Right, everybody. Welcome to the 142nd committee meeting of Hell.
Barry	Oh! I hate these! They're boring!
Scaramouche	You're meant to hate them – this is Hell!
Beelzebub	Exactly! It's not a summer holiday in Scarborough, you know. You're supposed to have a bad time.
Satan	Before we begin, I'd better make sure we're all here. *(Taking register)* Beelzebub?
Beelzebub	*(Raising hand)* Here.
Satan	Scaramouche?

Scaramouche	*(Raising hand)* Here.
Satan	Barry?
Barry	*(Raising hand and sounding bored)* Yes.
Satan	Right then – let's get started. I've called this meeting to discuss some very important business.
Barry	We haven't run out of toothpaste, have we?
Satan	No – there's been some new developments on earth which need our urgent attention. Something very strange has happened . . .
Scaramouche	Have England won a football match?
All	*(Jumping out of their seats)* What?!
Satan	No – God's given mankind ten commandments. He's told Moses to write them down on stone tablets. He wants mankind to obey them.
Beelzebub	What for, Satan?
Satan	To keep the human race faithful to him – and well away from us! That kind of rubbish.
Barry	So what are we going to do?
Satan	I want to draw up my own version – the Alternative Ten Commandments. Give God a bit of competition. *(Evil chuckle)*
Scaramouche	What did you have in mind?
Satan	We take the original ten – and use the complete opposite. For example, if God says black, we say white. If God says left, we say right. If God says blue, we say . . . er . . .
Beelzebub	Not blue?
Satan	Precisely, Beelzebub! Now the first commandment God gave is 'Worship No God Before Me.'
Barry	So what's your version?

Satan	*(Consulting Clipboard)* 'Worship Whoever You Like.' You see, if it's not God, it'll be me whatever they choose.
Scaramouche	I get it – money, work, posessions, people . . . ?
Satan	All Substitutes for God! Which leads very nicely on to my second commandment: 'Thou Shalt Make Idols.'
Barry	What sort of idols?
Satan	The usual stuff: Rolex watches, company cars, mobile phones, Cilla Black . . .
Beelzebub	Cilla Black's not an idol, Satan!
Barry	Yes she is – she's my idol! If I were on 'Blind Date' I wouldn't choose one of the contestants – I'd choose Cilla Black!
Satan	There we go then – she is an idol!
Scaramouche	*(Shrugging his shoulders)* God help her . . .
Satan	Ah! That's the next one: 'Thou Shalt Misuse the Name of God.'
Barry	How do you do that?
Beelzebub	Easy. Just say 'God' or 'Jesus' in the wrong context. Or maybe flippantly.
Scaramouche	Like . . . *(Wiping brow)* 'Thank God it's Friday!'
Beelzebub	Or . . . *(Shaking fist)* 'For God's sake!'
Satan	That's the spirit! Now – Number Four: 'Thou Shalt Ignore the Sabbath.' Go shopping instead. Work overtime. Watch telly all day. Spend all morning cooking Sunday lunch. Anything to avoid going to Church!
Barry	What's Number Five?
Satan	*(Consulting clipboard)* 'Thou Shalt Not Respect Thy Parents.'

Scaramouche	How about ignoring them? *(Evil chuckle)*
Beelzebub	Arguing with them? *(Evil chuckle)*
Barry	Baking them a delicious cake?
Satan, Scara & Beelzebub	*(Jumping out of their seats)* What?!!
Barry	And then eating it all yourself! *(Evil chuckle)*
Satan, Scara & Beelzebub	*(Wiping their brows)* Phew!
Satan	Excellent, lads – you're learning fast. Forget the fact that your parents gave you life, fed you, clothed you, cared for you. Treat them like dirt. *(Waving fist)* Let them know you really want to hurt them!
Barry	That sounds really nasty.
Scaramouche	It's meant to be – he's the Devil.
Beelzebub	He's not Noel Edmonds, you know – he's the Prince of Darkness. He's supposed to be evil.
Satan	*(Consulting clipboard)* Number Six: 'Thou Shalt Murder.' Remember, it needn't be a physical act. Just wishing someone were dead will do.
Scaramouche	*(Sneering)* How about character assassination? Killing someone's reputation?
Satan	Good one, Scaramouche! I love a bit of malicious gossip!
Beelzebub	What's Number Seven?
Satan	Well, I'd appreciate some help on this one . . . God came up with 'Thou Shalt Not Commit Adultery.' What do you reckon?

General head scratching. Deep thought. Whistling. Looking up at the ceiling and down at the floor. Embarrassed fidgeting. Etc.

Scaramouche	*(Raising hand)* Got it! 'Thou Shalt Commit Adultery!'
Satan, Barry & **Beelzebub**	Brilliant! *(They applaud)*
Beelzebub	Scaramouche – you're a genius!
Barry	Hang on! What if you're not married?
Satan	That's okay. Provided it's not your husband or wife, you can sleep with anyone you like. Any extra-marital sex will do the trick. *(Evil chuckle and rubbing his hands together)*
Beelzebub	Does wishing count?
Satan	Of course. Look at someone lustfully and you've sinned.
Barry	Oh dear. I do that all the time. I hope I don't go to Hell!
Scaramouche	Barry – you're already there.
Barry	Oh yeah. *(Pause)* Can I wish about Cilla Black?
Beelzebub	It's about the closest you'll ever get!
Satan	*(Consulting clipboard)* Number Eight: 'Thou Shalt Steal.'
Scaramouche	Steal what?
Satan	Whatever you like, Scaramouche. Objects, ideas, people, pencils from the stationery cupboard . . .
Beelzebub	Help yourself. Finders keepers. That kind of thing?
Satan	Precisely. Look after number one, that's what I say.

They all chuckle maliciously -- except for Barry.

Barry	*(Defensively)* I like that number one – it's got a really good tune . . . *(Starts singing whatever's number one in the Top 40 and waving his arms)*
Satan, Scara & **Beelzebub**	*(Turning to Barry)* Barry!
Barry	Sorry.

Satan	Number Nine: 'Thou Shalt Lie.' That includes cheating, misleading, exaggerating, and being economical with the truth.
Beelzebub	You can bend the truth!
Scaramouche	Like they do with statistics!
Satan	Exactly. They're some of the best-disguised lies.
Beelzebub	Hey, Barry. *(Adjusting hair)* Madonna thinks I'm really good looking.
Scaramouche	*(Flexing arm muscles)* And I had a fight with Arnold Swarzenegger.
Barry	Did you really?
Beelzebub	No – we're lying.
Barry	Doh!
Scaramouche	Which leaves Number Ten!
Barry	Is that 'Thou Shalt Not Eat Biscuits?'
Satan	No – God scrapped that one. Moses complained. He replaced it with . . . *(Consulting clipboard)* 'Thou Shalt Not Covet.'
Beelzebub	What have you come up with?
Barry	How about 'Thou Shalt Eat Biscuits?'
Satan	No – 'Thou Shalt Covet.' Basically, it's fine to be jealous, to envy, and to be greedy. It's all perfectly healthy and perfectly natural.
Scaramouche	I mean, we all need expensive trainers, don't we?
Beelzebub	And loads of records . . .
Satan	Not forgetting state-of-the-art computer games . . .
Barry	How about state-of-the-art biscuits?
Satan, Scara & **Beelzebub**	*(Turning to Barry)* Barry!
Barry	Sorry.
Scaramouche	So that's it?

Satan	That's it. The Alternative Ten Commandments!
Beelzebub	Who shall we get to spread them?
Scaramouche	I don't suppose Moses would be too interested . . .
Barry	We could put an advert in the local paper?
Satan	Listen – I've got a better idea. We'll get loads of people to spread them. The media, astrologers, New Age gurus – you name it.
Beelzebub	Hang on! No-one's going to follow these commandments. They're far too extreme.
Satan	*(Smiling)* I don't know . . . I think they're going to be extremely popular . . .

They break into an evil chuckle.

The World's Most Important Thing

This sketch should be a lot of fun, with plenty of audience participation, big gestures, and a quick tempo. As much as possible it should recreate the feel of a TV game show. The roles are exceptionally over-the-top and should be played as such. That way the downbeat ending becomes all the more effective.

As this piece is so long, do feel free to make any cuts you feel fit by omitting one or more of the characters interviewed.

Cast Cluffie Hook
Liz
Dave
Hartley Bigbucks
MC Gary
Dr Edith Chalmers
Heather

Props Spangly jacket
Calendar
2044 sign
Grey beard
Cardigan
Sock
Mobile phone
Bucket
Clock
Bananas
Plastic bag
Pineapple

Cluffie Hook bounds on-stage. He is just like an American gameshow host. He wears a spangly jacket and fakes an enormous smile. All his actions are exaggerated. He encourages the audience to react like a TV audience: clapping, cheering, and saying 'Aaaah' where appropriate.

Hook Hello – I'm Cluffie Hook and welcome to the Cluffie Hook show! Each week I set a prize question and my lucky contestants have to guess the correct answer. Last week I asked you to name the world's most loveliest person. And the answer was . . .
(Spreading his arms)

. . . me! This week I want to know – what is the world's most important thing? Remember – it must be something which can guarantee happiness and satisfaction always.
(Pause)
Let's meet today's first contestants.
(Cue applause)

Enter young couple – giggling and holding hands.

Dave   Hello, Cluffie.

Hook   Hi there. And who are you two?

Liz   I'm Liz – and this is Dave.

Hook   Great to have you on the show, folks! So what do you think is the world's most important thing?

Dave   We think it's romance.

Hook   And why's that?

Liz   Everyone knows why! Because love makes the world go round.

Dave   Love is purer than gold and sweeter than honey.

Liz   Love can climb mountains and cross oceans.

Dave   All you need is love.

Liz and Dave look romantically at each other – gazing into each other's eyes and sighing.

Hook   Okay, folks – let's see if Liz and Dave are right. We're going to whizz forward fifty years into the future and see how they get on. Here we go!

Loud, fast music bursts into life and everybody starts shaking. Liz and Dave run behind a screen/off-stage to do a quick change. Cluffie Hook takes a calendar and flicks over the days/months very rapidly. Finally he holds up a sign saying '2044'. Liz and Dave emerge from behind the screen. Their clothes are different. Dave has a grey beard and Liz is wearing a cardigan. They walk slower and scowl at each other.

Hook   They're back, ladies and gentlemen!
(Cue applause)
So, Liz and Dave, how did you get on?

Liz   Um. Not very well, actually.

Dave   We got divorced.

Hook   *(Amazed)*
                 How on earth did that happen? What went wrong?

Liz   After a short period of married bliss . . .

Dave   About four days . . .

Liz   We started arguing.

Dave   *(Miming squeezing toothpaste)*
                 She used to squeeze the toothpaste from the middle of
                 the tube – and I really hate that!

Liz   *(Holding up a sock)*
                 He used to leave dirty socks all over the house. That
                 really gets on my nerves! I mean, why can't he turn them
                 the right way out and stick them in the washing basket?
                 (Shrugs)

Hook   So, Liz and Dave: is romance the world's most important
                 thing?

Both   *(Shaking their heads)*
                 No.

Liz and Dave exit. Hook addresses the audience.

Hook   What a shame. So romance isn't the world's greatest
                 thing, ladies and gentlemen.
                 (Pause)
                 Time to meet our next contestant.
                 (Cue applause)

*Enter Hartley Bigbucks. He is dressed as a city businessman and talks
on a mobile phone.*

Bigbucks   *(Into phone)*
                 Sell Hanson, buy Eurotunnel, hold British Telecom!

Hook   Hello, contestant.

Bigbucks   *(Into phone)*
                 Okay, Josh – got to go! Send me a fax, will you?
                 (Puts phone away and shakes Hook's hand)
                 Ah, Mr. Hook. Delighted to meet you.

Hook   And your name, please?

73

Bigbucks	Bigbucks. Hartley Bigbucks. Chairman of Bigbucks PLC.
Hook	So, Mr Bigbucks – what do you think is the world's most important thing?
Bigbucks	Well, Mr Hook – I think it's success.
Hook	I see. And why's that?
Bigbucks	When you're successful, you can do anything. You can have first-class travel, posh restaurants, fancy parties, beautiful women – anything you want. Look at me: flash car, big house, mobile phone – I've got the lot! And people respect me. They think I'm the greatest. And do you know what? I am!
Hook	Okay, folks – let's see if Mr Bigbucks is right. Let's whizz forward fifty years.

Bigbucks goes behind the screen. Hook repeats the time-travel effect. Once again he finishes by holding up a sign saying '2044'. Bigbucks emerges in tatty clothes and carrying a bucket.

Hook	So, Mr Bigbucks – how did you get on?
Bigbucks	*(Embarrassed)* Er . . . Not too well, I'm afraid.
Hook	Go on.
Bigbucks	Well, my firm went into debt and I was made bankrupt. I lost my car, my house, my mobile phone – everything. All my friends ignore me, I can't afford first-class travel, and I haven't been to a party in over thirty years.
Hook	*(Grinning)* Never mind, Mr Bigbucks – I'm sure you'll bounce back.
Bigbucks	Well, I have started a new business. *(Lifts bucket and adopting Cockney accent)* Clean yer motor, Guv? Only a fiver!
Hook	So tell me, Hartley – is success the world's most important thing?
Bigbucks	*(Shakes head)* No. *(Exits)*

Hook   What a disappointment.
(Pause)
Time for another contestant.
(Cue applause)

Enter trendy raver. He is waving his arms and saying 'safe', 'respect', and 'nice one'. He is full of energy.

Hook   Hello there. And what's your name?

MC Gary   Yo, man! My name's MC Gary. Safe!

Hook   Right then, MC Gary. What do you think is the world's most important thing?

MC Gary   Oh, that's easy, man. Having a good time!

Hook   What do you mean?

MC Gary   You know – dancing, taking drugs, drinking loads of beer, hanging out with the babes. It's all about having a laugh – and being trendy.

Hook   Alright, MC Gary, it's time to whizz forward in time. Hold on tight, folks!

MC Gary goes behind the screen. Hook repeats the time-travel effect. This time he holds a clock and spins the hands very quickly. MC Gary re-emerges looking ill, skint, and depressed. He trudges on slowly – coughing and slurring his words.

Hook   Welcome back, MC Gary!

MC Gary   *(Sniffs)*
Alright.

Hook   So the big question – how did you get on?

MC Gary   Not too good, man. I'm broke, I've got no mates, I feel awful, and I'm not trendy.

Hook   So, is having a good time the world's most important thing?

MC Gary   *(Shaking head)*
No, man.
(He trudges off.)

Hook   Oh dear. Three contestants down – two to go. Let's bring on our next guest!
(Cue applause)

An extremely odd-looking woman comes on. She is carrying some bananas.

Hook   Hello, Madam.

Chalmers   Hello, Cluffie

Hook   And what's your name?

Chalmers   Dr Edith Chalmers, Professor in Applied Fruit, Oxford University.

Hook   And what do you think is the world's most important thing?

Chalmers   I believe the world's most important thing is the banana. *(Holds up bananas)*

Hook   *(Taken aback)*
        The banana?

Chalmers   That's right. The banana is an extremely popular fruit, rich in Vitamin C, with an attractive skin and a succulent flavour. What's more, the banana has mystical healing powers and the ability to speak French.

Hook   *(Bemused)*
        Right . . . Well, I think it's high time we whizzed you forward fifty years into the future.

Chalmers   Right-io.

The time-travel sequence is repeated. Chalmers goes behind the screen – only to emerge completely unchanged. She is carrying a plastic bag.

Hook   Welcome back, Dr Chalmers.

Chalmers   Crikey! That was quick!

Hook   So, Dr Chalmers – how did you get on with bananas?

Chalmers   *(Surprised)*
        Bananas?
        (Scornful)
        Oh – I've gone off bananas.

Hook   I'm sorry?

Chalmers   They're far too rich. And they go all black and squishy in your pocket. Worst of all, not once did a banana use its mystical healing powers nor did it speak French.
        (Shaking her head)
        Most disappointing.

Hook   So – bananas aren't the world's most important thing?

Chalmers   *(Shaking head)*
No.
(Removing a pineapple from the plastic bag and looking at it lovingly)
Pineapples are much better. Pineapples can solve complex mathematical equations and travel at the speed of light.

Hook   Dr Chalmers – thank you.

Chalmers   Thank you.

Dr Chalmers walks off, asking the pineapple some complex mathematical equations. Such as 'What is the square root of Pi?' or 'How does one calculate the hypotenuse of a right-angled triangle?'

Hook   *(Overly serious and melodramatic)*
So, only one contestant remaining. Will she find the correct answer? Here she is, ladies and gentlemen.
(Cue applause)

Enter Heather.

Hook   Hello, madam. And what's your name?

Heather   Hi – my name's Heather. Nice to be here.

Hook   Okay, Heather – you're our last hope. What do you think is the world's most important thing?

Heather   Well, I think it's following Jesus.

Hook   And why's that?

Heather   It's quite simple, really: because he created us, because he loves us, and because he died for us.
(Grins)
I don't recall a pineapple doing that . . .

Hook   You sound pretty sure of yourself, Heather. Let's zap forward fifty years into the future and see if you're right.

For the last time the time-travel effect is repeated. This time it's really manic and fast. Heather returns visibly older.

Hook   So, Heather, you're back with us. How did you get on?

Heather   Pretty well, thanks. The 2020s were a good laugh, but I had my fair share of ups and downs. It wasn't plain-sailing, Cluffie, but I'm still happy.

Hook   So, the $64,000 question: Heather, is following Jesus the world's most important thing?

Heather   *(Nodding enthusiastically)*
Oh yeah. Definitely. Following Jesus is more important than anything. Even pineapples!

Hook   *(Turning to audience)*
Well, folks. You've heard from Liz and Dave, Hartley Bigbucks, MC Gary, Dr Edith Chalmers, and Heather. Who had the right answer?
(Pause)
The choice . . .
(Points to audience)
. . . is yours.
(Pause)
That's all from me. This is Cluffie Hook saying goodbye – goodbye!
(Waves extravagantly and exits)

THE NATIONAL SOCIETY
A Christian Voice in Education

The National Society (Church of England) for Promoting Religious Education is a charity which supports all those involved in Christian education – teachers and school governors, students and parents, clergy and lay people – with the resources of its RE Centres, archives, courses and conferences.

Founded in 1811, the Society was chiefly responsible for setting up the nationwide network of Church schools in England and Wales and still provides grants for building projects and legal and administrative advice for headteachers and governors. It now publishes a wide range of books, pamphlets and audio-visual items, and two magazines, *Crosscurrent* and *Together*.

For details of membership of the Society or to receive a copy of our current catalogue please contact:

> The Promotions Secretary,
> The National Society,
> Church House,
> Great Smith Street,
> London
> SW1P 3NZ
> *Tel: 071-222 1672*